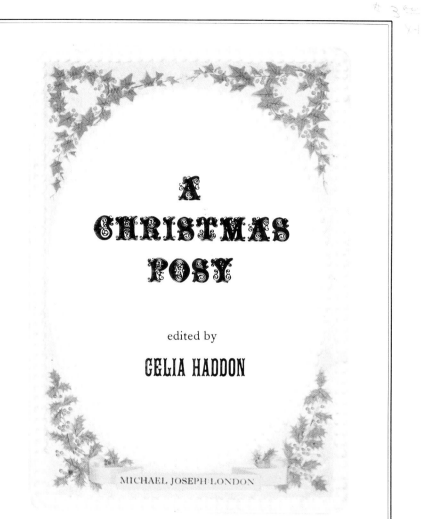

A CHRISTMAS POSY

edited by

CELIA HADDON

MICHAEL JOSEPH·LONDON

To
My Mother

MICHAEL JOSEPH LTD

Published by the Penguin Group
27 Wrights Lane, London W8 5TZ, England
Viking Penguin Inc., 40 West 23rd Street, New York, New York, 10010 USA
Penguin Books, Australia Ltd. Ringwood, Victoria, Australia
Penguin Books Canada Ltd. 2801 John Street, Markham Ontario, Canada L3R 1B4
Penguin Books (NZ) Ltd. 182-190 Wairau Road, Auckland 10, New Zealand

Penguin Books Ltd. Registered Offices Harmondsworth, Middlesex, England

First published November 1978
Second impression November 1978
Third impression November 1984
Fourth impression October 1988
Copyright © Celia Haddon 1978

Designed by Penny Mills
Made and printed in Singapore by
Kyodo Shing Loong Printing
A CIP catalogue record for this book is available from the British Library

ISBN 0 7181 1742 5

CONTENTS

[3]

A Merry Christmas

WELCOME CHRISTMAS

Now thrice welcome, Christmas,
Which brings us good cheer,
Minced pies and plum porridge,
Good ale and strong beer;
With pig, goose and capon,
The best that may be,
So well doth the weather
And our stomachs agree.

With holly and ivy,
So green and so gay,
We deck up our houses
As fresh as the day;
With bay and rosemary
And laurel complete;
And every one now
Is a king in conceit.

ANONYMOUS, 17th century.

THE OWL SONG

When icicles hang by the wall,
And Dick the shepherd blows his nail;
And Tom bears logs into the hall,
And milk comes frozen home in pail:
When blood is nipped, and ways be foul,
Then nightly sings the staring owl,
Tu-whit to-who.
A merry note,
While greasy Joan doth keel the pot.

When all aloud the wind doth blow,
And coughing drowns the parson's saw;
And birds sit brooding in the snow,
And Marian's nose looks red and raw:
When roasted crabs hiss in the bowl,
Then nightly sings the staring owl,
Tu-whit to-who.
A merry note,
While greasy Joan doth keel the pot.

WILLIAM SHAKESPEARE

GOD'S MOTHER

I sing of a maiden
That is makeless;
King of all kings
To her son she ches.

He came all so still
Where his mother was
As dew in April
That falleth on the grass.

He came all so still
Where his mother lay
As dew in April
That falleth on the spray.

He came all so still
To his mother's bower
As dew in April
That falleth on the flower.

Mother and maiden
Was never none but she;
Well may such a lady
Godes mother be.

ANONYMOUS, 15th century.

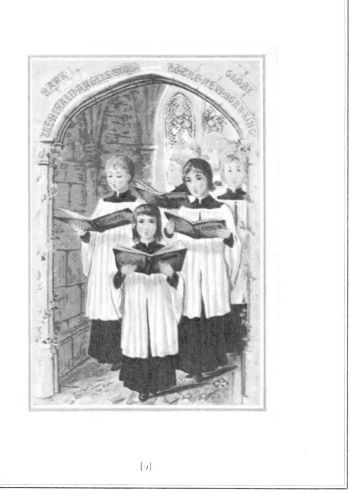

Soft Snow

I walked abroad in a snowy day:
I ask'd the soft snow with me to play:
She play'd and she melted in all her prime,
And the winter call'd it a dreadful crime.

WILLIAM BLAKE

THE COMPLIMENTS OF THE SEASON

Schoolboys in Winter

The schoolboys still their morning rambles take
To neighbouring village school with playing speed,
Loitering with pastime's leisure till they quake,
Oft looking up the wild-geese droves to heed,
Watching the letters which their journeys make;
Or plucking haws on which the fieldfares feed,
And hips, and sloes; and on each shallow lake
Making glib slides, where they like shadows go
Till some fresh pastimes in their minds awake.
Then off they start anew and hasty blow
Their numbed and clumpsing fingers till they glow;
Then races with their shadows wildly run
That stride huge giants o'er the shining snow
In the pale splendour of the winter sun.

JOHN CLARE

GLORY TO THE KING. NEW-BORN

HYMN ON CHRIST'S NATIVITY

It was the winter wild,
While the heaven-born child
All meanly wrapt in the rude manger lies;
Nature, in awe to him,
Had doff'd her gaudy trim,
With her great Master so to sympathise:
It was no season then for her
To wanton with the sun, her lusty paramour.

Ring out, ye crystal spheres;
Once bless our human ears,
If ye have power to touch our senses so;
And let your silver chime
Move in melodious time;
And let the bass of Heaven's deep organ blow;
And, with your ninefold harmony,
Make up full consort to the angelic symphony.

But see, the Virgin blest
Hath laid her Babe to rest:
Time is, our tedious song should here have ending:
Heaven's youngest-teemed star
Hath fix'd her polish'd car,
Her sleeping Lord with handmaid lamp attending:
And all about the courtly stable
Bright-harness'd angels sit in order serviceable.

JOHN MILTON

A Blessing

God bless the master of this house,
The mistress also,
And all the little children
That round the table go:

And all your kin and kinsfolk,
That dwell both far and near;
I wish you a merry Christmas
And a happy new year.

ANONYMOUS, 17th century.

ANTICIPATION

A WINTER EVENING

Now stir the fire, and close the shutters fast,
Let fall the curtains, wheel the sofa round,
And, while the bubbling and loud hissing urn
Throws up a steamy column, and the cups,
That cheer but not inebriate, wait on each,
So let us welcome peaceful ev'ning in . . . .

O Winter, ruler of th'inverted year,
Thy scatter'd hair with sleet like ashes fill'd,
Thy breath congeal'd upon thy lips, thy cheeks
Fring'd with a beard made white with other snows
Than those of age, thy forehead wrapp'd in clouds,
A leafless branch thy sceptre, and thy throne
A sliding car, indebted to no wheels,
But urg'd by storms along its slipp'ry way,
I love thee, all unlovely as thou seem'st,
And dreaded as thou art! . . .

I crown thee king of intimate delights,
Fire-side enjoyments, homeborn happiness,
And all the comforts, that the lowly roof
Of undisturb'd Retirement and the hours
Of long uninterrupted ev'ning know.

WILLIAM COWPER

THE BURNING BABE

As I in hoary winter's night stood shivering in the snow,
Surprised I was with sudden heat which made my heart to
      glow;
And lifting up a fearful eye to view what fire was near,
A pretty Babe all burning bright did in the air appear;
Who, scorched with excessive heat, such floods of tears did
      shed,
As though his floods should quench his flames which with his
      tears were fed.
"Alas!" quoth he, "but newly born in fiery heats I fry,
Yet none approach to warm their hearts or feel my fire but I.
My faultless breast the furnace is, the fuel wounding thorns;
Love is the fire, and sighs the smoke, the ashes shame and
      scorns;
The fuel Justice layeth on, and Mercy blows the coals;
The metal in this furnace wrought are men's defiled souls;
For which, as now on fire I am to work them to their good,
So will I melt into a bath to wash them in my blood."
With this he vanished out of sight and swiftly shrunk away,
And straight I called unto mind that it was Christmas Day.

ROBERT SOUTHWELL.

MANY A HAPPY CHRISTMAS MAY YOU ENJOY

A MERRIE CHRISTMASSE UNDER THE MISTLETOE

Old Christmas

And well our Christian sires of old
Loved when the year its course had rolled,
And brought blithe Christmas back again,
With all his hospitable train.

The damsel donned her kirtle sheen;
The hall was dressed with holly green;
Forth to the wood did merry-men go,
To gather in the mistletoe.
Then opened wide the baron's hall
To vassal, tenant, serf, and all;
Power laid his rod of rule aside,
And Ceremony doffed his pride.
The heir with roses in his shoes,
That night might village partner chuse;
The lord, underogating, share
The vulgar game of "post and pair".

England was merry England, when
Old Christmas brought his sports again.
'Twas Christmas broached the mightiest ale;
'Twas Christmas told the merriest tale;
A Christmas gambol oft could cheer
The poor man's heart through half the year.

WALTER SCOTT

WISHING YOU A HAPPY CHRISTMAS

In Him dwelleth all the fulness
of the God-head bodily

Christmas at Sea

The sheets were frozen hard, and they cut the naked hand;
The decks were like a slide, where a seaman scarce could stand;
The wind was a nor'wester, blowing squally off the sea;
And cliffs and spouting breakers were the only things a-lee.

They heard the surf a-roaring before the break of day;
But 'twas only with the peep of light we saw how ill we lay.
We tumbled every hand on deck instanter, with a shout,
And we gave her the maintops'l ,and stood by to go about.

All day we tacked and tacked between the South Head and the North;
All day we hauled the frozen sheets, and go no further forth;
All day as cold as charity, in bitter pain and dread,
For very life and nature we tacked from head to head.

We gave the South a wider berth, for there the tide-race roared;
But every tack we made we brought the North Head close aboard;
So's we saw the cliffs and houses, and the breakers running high,
And the coastguard in his garden, with his glass against his eye.

The frost was on the village roofs as white as ocean foam;
The good red fires were burning bright in every 'longshore home;
The windows sparkled clear, and the chimneys volleyed out;
And I vow we sniffed the victuals and the vessel went about.

The bells upon the church were rung with a mighty jovial cheer
For it's just that I should tell you how (of all days in the year)
This day of our adversity was blessed Christmas morn,
And the house above the coastguard's was the house where I was born.

O well I saw the pleasant room, the pleasant faces there,
My mother's silver spectacles, my father's silver hair;
And well I saw the firelight, like a flight of homely elves,
Go dancing round the china-plates that stand upon the shelves.

And well I knew the talk they had, the talk that was of me,
Of the shadow on the household and the son that went to sea;
And O the wicked fool I seemed, in every kind of way,
To be here and hauling frozen ropes on blessed Christmas Day.

They lit the high sea-light, and the dark began to fall.
"All hands to loose topgallant sails", I heard the captain call.
"By the Lord, she'll never stand it," our first mate, Jackson, cried.
"It's the one way or the other, Mr Jackson," he replied.

She staggered to her bearings, but the sails were new and good.
And the ship smelt up to windward just as though she understood.
As the winter's day was ending, in the entry of the night,
We cleared the weary headland, and passed below the light.

And they heaved a mighty breath, every soul on board but me,
As they saw her nose again pointing handsome out to sea;
But all that I could think of, in the darkness and the cold
Was just that I was leaving home and my folks were growing old.

ROBERT LOUIS STEVENSON

LOVE

So, the year's done with!
(*Love me for ever!*)
All March begun with,
April's endeavour;
May-wreaths that bound me
June needs must sever;
Now snows fall around me,
Quenching June's fever—
(*Love me for ever!*)

ROBERT BROWNING

Merry Christmas and a Happy New Year.

THE VIRGIN'S CRADLE HYMN

Sleep, sweet babe! my cares beguiling:
Mother sits beside thee smiling;
Sleep, my darling, tenderly!
If thou sleep not, mother mourneth,
Singing as her wheel she turneth:
Come, soft slumber, balmily!

SAMUEL COLERIDGE

A BRIGHT AND HAPPY CHRISTMAS

A CRADLE HYMN

Hush! my dear, lie still and slumber,
Holy angels guard thy bed!
Heavenly blessings without number
Gently falling on thy head.

Sleep, my babe; thy food and raiment,
House and home thy friends provide;
All without thy care or payment,
All thy wants are well supply'd.

How much better thou'rt attended
Than the Son of God could be,
When from heaven He descended
And became a child like thee!

Soft and easy is thy cradle:
Coarse and hard thy Saviour lay;
When His birth-place was a stable,
And His softest bed was hay.

Lo, He slumbers in His manger,
Where the horned oxen fed;
Peace, my darling, here's no danger,
Here's no ox a-near thy bed.

'Twas to save thee, child, from dying,
Save my dear from burning flame,
Bitter groans and endless crying
That thy blest Redeemer came.

ISAAC WATTS

[27]

FROST AT MIDNIGHT

The Frost performs its secret ministry,
Unhelped by any wind. The owlet's cry
Came loud – and hark, again! loud as before.
The inmates of my cottage, all at rest,
Have left me to that solitude, which suits
Abstruser musings: save that at my side
My cradled infant slumbers peacefully.
'Tis calm indeed! so calm, that it disturbs
And vexes meditation with its strange
And extreme silentness. Sea, hill, and wood,
This populous village! Sea, and hill, and wood,
With all the numberless goings-on of life,
Inaudible as dreams! the thin blue flame
Lies on my low-burnt fire, and quivers not;
Only that film, which fluttered on the grate,
Still flutters there, the sole unquiet thing.
Methinks its motion in this hush of nature
Gives it dim sympathies with me who live,
Making it a companionable form,
Whose puny flaps and freaks the idling Spirit
By its own moods interprets, everywhere
Echo or mirror seeking of itself,
And makes a toy of Thought . . .

SAMUEL COLERIDGE.

A Visit from St Nicholas

"Twas the night before Christmas, when all through the house
Not a creature was stirring, not even a mouse;
The stockings were hung by the chimney with care,
In hopes that St Nicholas soon would be there;
The children were nestled all snug in their beds,
While visions of sugar-plums danced in their heads;
And mamma in her 'kerchief, and I in my cap,
Had just settled our brains for a long winter's nap,
When out on the lawn there arose such a clatter,
I sprang from the bed to see what was the matter.
Away to the window I flew like a flash,
Tore open the shutters and threw up the sash.
The moon on the breast of the new-fallen snow
Gave the lustre of mid-day to objects below,
When, what to my wondering eyes should appear,
But a miniature sleigh, and eight tiny reindeer,
With a little old driver, so lively and quick,
I knew in a moment it must be St. Nick.
More rapid than eagles his coursers they came,
And he whistled, and shouted, and called them by name;
"Now *Dasher*! now, *Dancer*! now *Prancer* and *Vixen*!
On, *Comet*! on, *Cupid*! on, *Donder* and *Blitzen*!
To the top of the porch! to the top of the wall!
Now dash away! dash way! dash away all!"
As dry leaves that before the wild hurricane fly,
When they meet with an obstacle, mount to the sky;
So up to the house-top the coursers they flew,
With a sleigh full of toys, and St Nicholas too.

CLEMENT CLARKE MOORE

WISHING YOU A MERRY CHRISTMAS.

Cauld
Blaws the Wind

Cauld blaws the wind frae east to west,
The drift is driving sairly,
Sae loud and shill's I hear the blast—
I'm sure it's winter fairly.

Up in the morning's no for me,
Up in the morning early!
When a' the hills are cover'd wi' snaw,
I'm sure it's winter fairly!

The birds sit chittering in the thorn,
A' day they fare but sparely,
And lang's the night frae e'en to morn—
I'm sure it's winter fairly.

ROBERT BURNS

A MERRY CHRISTMAS TO YOU

MAKE WE MERRY

Make we merry, both more and less,
For now is the time of Christmas!

Let no man come into this hall,
Groom, page, nor yet marshall,
But that some sport he bring withal!
For now is the time of Christmas!

If that he say he cannot sing,
Some other sport then let him bring,
That it may please at this feasting.
For now is the time of Christmas!

If he say he can nought do,
Then for my love ask him no mo,
But to the stocks then let him go!
For now is the time of Christmas!

ANONYMOUS, 16th century

A Merry Christmas and a Happy New Year.

A MERRY CHRISTMAS & A HAPPY NEW YEAR.

THE ROBIN

Art thou the bird whom man loves best,
The pious bird with the scarlet breast,
Our little English robin;
The bird that comes about our doors
When autumn winds are sobbing?
The bird who by some name or other
All men who know thee call their brother?

WILLIAM WORDSWORTH

THE ROSE

There is no rose of such virtue
As is the rose that bare Jesu.
Alleluia

For in this rose contained was
Heaven and earth in little space
Res miranda

By that rose we may well see
There be one God in persons three,
Pares forma.

The angels sungen the shepherds to
Gloria in excelsis Deo.
Gaudeamus

Leave we all this wordly mirth
And follow we this joyful birth.
Transeamus.

ANONYMOUS, 15th century

WISHING YOU A JOYOUS CHRISTMAS AND
A HAPPY NEW YEAR.

Though Winter's breath to swift destruction doometh
Terrestrial flowers that smile in summer-time,
The Rose of Charity for ever bloometh,
And Christmas sees it in its glorious prime.

Nowel, Nowel, Nowel, Nowel

Nowel, nowel, nowel, nowel,
Tidings good I think to tell.
The boares head that we bring here
Betokeneth a prince withouten peer
Is born this day to buy us dear.
        Nowel.

A boar is a sovereign beast
And acceptable in every feast:
So must this Lord be to most and least.
        Nowel.

The boares head we bring with song
In worship of Him that thus sprung
Of a virgin, to redress all wrong.
        Nowel.

ANONYMOUS, 16th century

A
Merry Christmas
and a
happy new year

CHRISTMAS NIGHT

Some say, that ever 'gainst that season comes
Wherein our Saviour's birth is celebrated,
The bird of dawning singeth all night long:
And then, they say, no spirit can walk abroad;
The nights are wholesome; then no planets strike,
No fairy takes, nor witch hath power to charm,
So hallow'd and so gracious is the time.

WILLIAM SHAKESPEARE

A Merry Christmas.

A WINTER PIECE

And yet but lately have I seen, e'en here,
The Winter in a lovely dress appear.

For ev'ry shrub, and ev'ry blade of grass,
And ev'ry pointed thorn, seem'd wrought in glass.
In pearls and rubies rich the hawthorns show,
While thro' the ice the crimson berries glow.
The thick-sprung reeds the watry marshes yield,
Seem polish'd lances in a hostile field.
The stag in limpid currents with surprize
Sees chrystal branches on his forehead rise.
The spreading oak, the beech, and tow'ring pine,
Glaz'd over, in the freezing aether shine.
The frighted birds the rattling branches shun,
That wave and glitter in the distant sun.
When if a sudden gust of wind arise,
The brittle forest into atoms flies:
The crackling wood beneath the tempest bends,
And in a spangled show'r the prospect ends.

AMBROSE PHILIPS

THE HOLLY BOUGH

Ye who have scorn'd each other,
Or injured friend or brother,
In this fast-fading year;
Ye who, by word or deed,
Have made a kind heart bleed,
Come gather here.

Let sinn'd-against and sinning
Forget their strife's beginning,
And join in friendship now;
Be links no longer broken;
Be sweet forgiveness spoken
Under the holly bough.

Ye who have loved each other,
Sister and friend and brother,
In this fast-fading year;
Mother and sire and child,
Young man and maiden mild,
Come gather here;

And let your hearts grow fonder,
As memory shall ponder
Each past unbroken vow.
Old love and younger wooing
Are sweet in the renewing
Under the holly bough.

CHARLES MACKAY

A HAPPY CHRISTMAS

[46]

NEW YEAR BELLS

Ring out, wild bells, to the wild sky,
The flying cloud, the frosty light:
The year is dying in the night;
Ring out, wild bells, and let him die.

Ring out the old, ring in the new,
Ring, happy bells, across the snow:
The year is going, let him go;
Ring out the false, ring in the true.

Ring out the grief that saps the mind,
For those that here we see no more;
Ring out the feud of rich and poor,
Ring in redress to all mankind.

Ring out old shapes of foul disease;
Ring out the narrowing lust of gold;
Ring out the thousand wars of old,
Ring in the thousand years of peace.

Ring in the valiant man and free,
The larger heart, the kindlier hand;
Ring out the darkness of the land,
Ring in the Christ that is to be.

ALFRED TENNYSON

NEW YEAR'S WISH.

May joy and peace e'er
be with thee,
And happiness attend
thy way;
May brighter still thy
prospects be,
On each succeeding
New Year's Day.

The editor wishes to express gratitude to The Mansell Collection and to the Mary Evans Picture Library for pictures reproduced in this book.

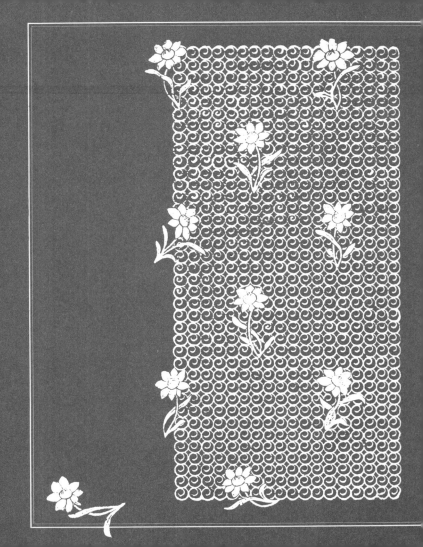